A GLASS CEILING SURVEY

BENCHMARKING BARRIERS AND PRACTICES

A GLASS CEILING SURVEY

BENCHMARKING BARRIERS AND PRACTICES

Ann M. Morrison
Carol T. Schreiber
Karl F. Price

Center for Creative Leadership
Greensboro, North Carolina

The Center for Creative Leadership is an international, nonprofit educational institution founded in 1970 to foster leadership and effective management for the good of society overall. As a part of this mission, it publishes books and reports that aim to contribute to a general process of inquiry and understanding in which ideas related to leadership are raised, exchanged, and evaluated. The ideas presented in its publications are those of the author or authors.

The Center thanks you for supporting its work through the purchase of this volume. If you have comments, suggestions, or questions about any Center publication, please contact Walter W. Tornow, Vice President, Research and Publication, at the address given below.

Center for Creative Leadership
Post Office Box 26300
Greensboro, North Carolina 27438-6300

CENTER FOR CREATIVE LEADERSHIP

©1995 Center for Creative Leadership

All rights reserved. No part of this publication may be reproduced, stored in a retrieval system, or transmitted, in any form or by any means, electronic, mechanical, photocopying, recording, or otherwise, without the prior written permission of the publisher. Printed in the United States of America.

CCL No. 161

Library of Congress Cataloging-in-Publication Data

Morrison, Ann M.
    A glass ceiling survey : benchmarking barriers and practices / Ann M. Morrison, Carol T. Schreiber, Karl F. Price.
        p. cm.
    Includes bibliographical references.
    ISBN 1-882197-10-0
    1. Women executives—United States. 2. Minority executives—United States.
 I. Schreiber, Carol Tropp. II. Price, Karl F. III. Title.
HD6054.4.U6M673 1995
331.4'816584'00973—dc20   95-35392
                                                                                     CIP

Table of Contents

Foreword vii
Acknowledgments ix
Introduction 1
Method 1
   Survey 1
   Participants 2
   Procedure 3
Results and Discussion 3
   The Importance of Diversity 8
   How Effective Are Organizations in Achieving Diversity? 10
   Top Barriers to Advancement 11
      Comparison to GOLD Project 12
      Differences in top barriers 14
      Summary 15
   Key Practices 16
      The most prevalent diversity practices 17
      The most critical diversity practices 18
      Practices associated with two key diversity barriers 19
         Lower "discomfort" barrier 19
         Lower "lack of accountability" barrier 21
      Practices most closely associated with overall effectiveness 23
      The most significant diversity practice 26
      Implications of key practices for organizations wishing to implement them 27
References 31
Appendix: Survey Questions and Responses 33

Foreword

In 1992 the Human Resource Planning Society and the Center for Creative Leadership launched a cooperative research project called the Glass Ceiling Benchmark Survey. The project's purpose was to build on an earlier CCL research project—Guidelines on Leadership Diversity (GOLD)—and further assess the current state of organizational practices in support of workforce diversity.

This research collaboration had many benefits. First, the effort represented a long-standing interest of both organizations in the topic of diversity. Second, it allowed for a complementation of research methodologies. The Center's GOLD Project was qualitative in nature, based on in-depth interviews with about 200 managers in sixteen model organizations. The benchmark survey provided an opportunity to extend the Center's research by quantitatively examining the state of the practice in a larger sample of organizations.

We hope to undertake similar collaborative efforts, with HRPS and with other organizations, in the future.

Walter W. Tornow
Vice President, Research and Publication
October 1995

Acknowledgments

The Glass Ceiling Benchmark Survey was jointly sponsored by the Human Resource Planning Society and the Center for Creative Leadership. Funding was provided through a grant from HRPS. The authors of this CCL report, one outcome of the survey research, thank Walter W. Tornow of CCL and Normand W. Green of HRPS for their assistance and support.

Introduction

Nontraditional managers (white women, native-born people of color, and immigrants) are in the workforce in greater numbers than ever before, and their presence is predicted to rise (Johnston & Packer, 1987). Yet their increased numbers have not been matched by a corresponding rise in their representation in senior levels of management. This phenomenon, referred to as *the glass ceiling,* presents a challenge to organizations: that of identifying the barriers to the upward mobility of nontraditional managers and implementing practices that successfully overcome these barriers.

In the Guidelines on Leadership Diversity (GOLD) Project, the Center for Creative Leadership (CCL) conducted in-depth interviews with nearly 200 managers in sixteen organizations (businesses, educational institutions, and government agencies) recognized for their exemplary diversity programs (see Morrison, 1992). They were asked what barriers existed to prevent nontraditional managers from reaching higher-level ranks of management and what key policies and practices were used to overcome these barriers.

In 1992 the Human Resource Planning Society (HRPS) and CCL undertook a companion project, the Glass Ceiling Benchmark Survey, which looked at a larger sample of organizations and focused on some of the issues raised in the GOLD Project research: (1) the importance of diversity to their organizations; (2) the effectiveness of their organizations in achieving diversity in the workforce; (3) the effect of barriers on the upward mobility of nontraditional managers; and (4) the prevalence, importance, and effectiveness of key practices for supporting workforce diversity. This report documents the results of that survey and compares some of these findings with those from the GOLD Project.

This report is for organizational leaders, human resources professionals, and other individuals concerned with developing diversity in their organizations at the management level. It provides a framework of ideas for approaching the task of identifying barriers and implementing key practices.

Method

Survey

With the GOLD Project issues in mind, we developed an eleven-question survey in the spring of 1992. (See the Appendix for a complete list of survey questions and their results.) The first seven questions were:

Question 1. How important is a diverse workforce to your organization in terms of such things as increasing productivity, reducing employee turnover, increasing creativity, "It's the right thing to do," and so forth?

Question 2. Of the reasons for workforce diversity listed in question 1, which is most important to your organization?

Question 3. Given all of the issues facing your organization, how important is the issue of workforce diversity?

Question 4. How important are the thirty-nine diversity practices listed here to your executive and management ranks? To what extent is your organization developing, implementing, or evaluating these practices? How effective have these practices been when fully implemented?

Question 5. To what extent do the barriers to achieving diversity identified in *The New Leaders* (Morrison, 1992) currently exist in your executive and management ranks?

Question 6. Overall, how effective has your organization been in achieving diversity in your workforce, management ranks, and executive ranks?

Question 7. During the past five years, how has the opportunity for promotions changed within your organization's management ranks?

The four remaining questions asked for demographic information on the respondents.

Participants

A mailing list of 902 human resources managers was compiled from the major U.S.-based corporations on the HRPS membership list, along with a variety of not-for-profit, government, and education organizations on the CCL client list. Human resources managers were selected as respondents because they are often the principal contact in the organization for diversity issues (as opposed to a line manager, for example), and these issues are typically in their bailiwick.

Large industrial and service firms tend to dominate the sample. (See questions 8, 9, and 10 in the Appendix for exact statistics.) Of the 304 organizations, 109 are from the Fortune 1000 list, including 71 from the Fortune 500 Industrials and 24 from the Fortune 50. Overall, manufacturing and service companies were about equally represented (45% and 42% of the sample, respectively); only 13% of the sample was comprised of not-for-profit organizations. The majority of organizations surveyed employed more than 5,000 employees.

Seventy-nine percent of the respondents reported on their total organization, and 21% reported on a division or other unit of a larger organization. Participating organizations varied in size: fewer than 1,000 employees (19%); 1,000 to 4,999 employees (26%); 5,000 to 9,999 employees (15%); 10,000 to 24,999 employees (17%); and 25,000 or more employees (23%). No information was collected on the individual respondents.

Procedure

Surveys were mailed in early June 1992, and 304 responses were received by the end of July, for a 34% response rate. Initial analyses of the survey responses began in September 1992. The responses were counted and converted into percentages, and correlations with barriers and effectiveness were completed. A report of initial findings was sent to all survey participants who requested one in December 1992 (Human Resource Planning Society/Center for Creative Leadership, 1992).

Results and Discussion

The most important results of the survey, which are drawn from the first seven questions, are described in Table 1 (complete text and results for each question are in the Appendix).

The following discussion is organized around the four research issues given in the "Introduction": Thus, we begin with an analysis of the importance data from the 304 organizations studied; look at the overall effectiveness of diversity initiatives in executive ranks, management ranks, and the general workforce of the organizations studied; continue with a consideration of the barriers that impede upward mobility for nontraditional managers in these organizations, including comparative data from the GOLD Project; and address the top diversity practices found in this survey in terms of their importance, usage, and effectiveness, and cite comparative data (the top-ten practices) from the GOLD Project.

Parts of the discussion deal with similarities and differences between the findings of this survey and those of the GOLD Project, particularly in the sections on barriers and practices. Thus, it is useful to be aware of the differences between the two studies. First, the GOLD Project was conducted in organizations selected for their excellence in diversity practices. The Glass Ceiling Benchmark Survey participant organizations were chosen from CCL and HRPS mailing lists and represent a spectrum of experience (from broad

Table 1
Glass Ceiling Benchmark Survey: Highlights of Findings

Question 1: How important is a diverse workforce to your organization?

Of 16 suggested reasons—which could be rated as important, somewhat important, neither important nor unimportant, somewhat unimportant, or unimportant—the following were most often rated as important: "Enlarging pool of management talent" (by 49% of those responding), "Enlarging pool of executive talent" (47%), "Facilitating recruiting" (45%), and "It's the right thing to do" (45%).

Question 2: Of the reasons for workforce diversity listed in question 1, which is most important to your organization?

The following were most often rated as most important: "Enhancing competitiveness" (by 17% of those responding), "It's the right thing to do" (13%), "Enlarging pool of management talent" (11%), and "Meeting government regulations" (9%).

The following were least often rated as important: "Reducing costs" (by 1% of those responding), "Reducing employee turnover" (1%), "Enlarging pool of executive talent" (2%), and "Improving decision making" (2%).

Question 3: Given all of the issues facing your organization, how important is the issue of workforce diversity?

Of those responding, 44% rated the issue as somewhat important, 29% important, 15% neither important nor unimportant, 9% somewhat important, and 3% unimportant.

Question 4.1: Please indicate, in terms of achieving diversity in your executive and management talent, how important the practices listed here are.

Of 39 suggested practices—which could be rated as important, somewhat important, neither important nor unimportant, somewhat unimportant, or unimportant—the following were most often rated as important: "Organization has policies against racism, sexism" (by 83% of those responding), "Organization has grievance procedure or complaint resolution process" (68%), "Development programs exist for all

Table 1 (continued)

high-potential managers" (56%), and "Organization has work and family policies" (52%).

Question 4.2: Please indicate, in terms of achieving diversity in your executive and management talent, the extent to which your organization is developing, implementing, or evaluating each of the practices listed here:

Of 39 suggested practices—which could be rated as tried and abandoned, already fully implemented, implementation under way, under development, being evaluated, or not addressed, the following practices were most often rated as already fully implemented: "Organization has policies against racism, sexism" (by 85% of those responding), "Organization has grievance procedures or complaint resolution process" (76%), "Organization sponsors access to external training and seminars" (69%), "Organization has active AA/EEO Committee/Office" (61%).

The following practices were most often rated as implementation underway: "Top management provides resources to support workforce diversity (e.g., space, time, money)" (by 32% of those responding), "Organization has work and family policies" (27%), "Top management personally intervenes to encourage and reward managers to pursue diversity goals" (26%), and "Top management publicly and repeatedly advocates diversity both inside and outside the organization" (26%).

The following practices were most often rated as under development: "Top management personally intervenes to encourage and reward managers to pursue diversity goals" (by 20% of those responding), "Top management publicly and repeatedly advocates diversity both inside and outside the organization" (18%), "Top management provides resources to support workforce diversity (e.g., space, time, money)" (17%), and "Diversity considerations are included in management succession planning" (17%).

The following practices were most often rated as being evaluated: "Organization uses a formal mentoring program" (by 23% of those responding), "Entry-level development program exists for identified high-potential employees" (18%), "Top management personally intervenes to encourage and reward managers to pursue diversity goals" (17%), "Child-care resources are available" (17%), and "Competence in managing a diverse workforce is considered in management succession planning" (17%).

Table 1 (continued)

The following practices were most often rated as not addressed: "Achieving diversity goals is recognized through events and awards" (by 71% of those responding), "Development programs exist specifically for women and people of color identified as having high potential" (62%), "Progress on diversity goals is included in determining managers' compensation" (55%), "Internal training programs exist for women and people of color" (51%), and "Organization's diversity efforts are given extensive public exposure" (51%).

Question 4.3: Please indicate, for those practices that are rated as fully implemented, how effective the practices have been.

Of the practices fully implemented—which could be rated as very effective, largely effective, neither effective nor ineffective, somewhat effective, or ineffective—the following were rated as very effective: "Organization uses an internship program" (by 21% of those responding), "Organization has partnerships with educational institutions (e.g., high schools, technical schools, college teachers)" (21%), "Organization has partnerships with nontraditional groups (e.g., National Urban League, black or Hispanic MBA associations)" (21%), and "Key outside mid-career hires are used to enhance diversity" (18%).

The following were rated as somewhat effective: "Organization has an active AA/EEO Committee/Office" (by 49% of those responding), "Selection criteria and decisions include diversity considerations" (46%), "Organization has work and family policies" (45%), and "Organization provides diversity training programs" (44%).

Question 5: To what extent do each of the following barriers to achieving diversity currently exist in your executive and managerial ranks?

Of 18 suggested barriers—which could be rated as exists to a great extent, exists to a moderate extent, exists to a small extent, exists to a slight extent, or does not exist—the following were rated as exists to a great extent: "Traditional managers (white males) are already in place, limiting access to women and people of color because they have greater comfort with their own kind" (by 37% of those responding), "Lack of accountability or incentives for diversity" (35%), "Business restrictions (such as downsizing)" (23%), and "Inertia, risk-averse culture" (20%).

Table 1 (continued)

The following were rated as does not exist: "Pay differentials" (by 59% of those responding), "Cannot find qualified candidates who are women or people of color because they are unwilling to relocate" (45%), "Cannot find qualified candidates who are women or people of color because they have difficulty balancing work and family" (45%), and "Isolating community environment" (38%).

Question 6.1: Overall, how effective has your organization been in achieving diversity in your workforce?

Given the possible ratings of very effective, largely effective, somewhat effective, slightly effective, or ineffective, respondents rated their organizations as follows: very effective (16%), largely effective (34%), and ineffective (4%).

Question 6.2: Overall, how effective has your organization been in achieving diversity in your management ranks?

Given the possible ratings described above, respondents rated their organizations as follows: very effective (3%), largely effective (10%), and ineffective (13%).

Question 6.3: Overall, how effective has your organization been in achieving diversity in your executive ranks?

Given the possible ratings described above, respondents rated their organizations as follows: very effective (4%), largely effective (3%), and ineffective (49%).

Question 7: During the past five years, how has the opportunity for promotions changed within your organization's management ranks?

Given the possible ratings of declined significantly, declined somewhat, stayed about the same, increased somewhat, and increased significantly, respondents rated their organizations as follows: declined significantly (19%), declined somewhat (32%), and stayed about the same (23%).

to very little) with diversity initiatives. Second, the participants interviewed in the GOLD Project were a heterogeneous group of managers and executives in terms of their functions; the managers and executives in the Glass Ceiling Benchmark Survey were strictly human resources professionals. Third, the first study included data from only sixteen organizations (197 individuals), and the second study included data from 304 organizations. Fourth, the information was gathered by interview in the first study and by survey in the second. Finally, the questions asked in the second study were not identical to those in the first. Although they were based on them, their emphases were different. Whereas the GOLD Project concentrated on identifying barriers and effective practices, the Glass Ceiling Benchmark Survey focused on determining the importance of diversity efforts to the organization and the extent to which such practices reduced barriers at various levels.

Whenever specific questions or results are discussed, the reader is referred to the particular question in the Appendix for a complete overview or to Table 1 for the highlights.

The Importance of Diversity

Responses to survey question 3 indicate some reluctance by these human resources managers to make diversity a priority. Only 29% said diversity is important. Another 44% rated diversity as somewhat important, which is encouraging; but other issues, if they had been included in this survey, could also have been rated as more important. The survey responses are not clear on how important diversity issues are relative to other business issues.

Other studies have shown that diversity is ranked low on lists of organizational priorities. A 1990 survey of readers of *Training and Development* (1991), for example, found that workforce diversity ranked low in interest. It ranked 12 on a list of 14 issues, with an interest rating of 62 on a scale of 1 to 100. A 1992 survey by the Hay Group (Rigdon, 1992) also revealed a lack of concern about workforce diversity. Nearly two-thirds of the 1,405 companies responding indicated that adapting to workforce diversity is either important but not a priority (44%) or not very important (20%) for the next two years.

The reasons given by the participants in the Glass Ceiling Benchmark Survey for the importance of diversity are surprising. We surmised that this was because perhaps they were not yet aware of the benefits that diversity could contribute to their businesses. For instance in question 1, managers were asked *why* diversity rates at least some importance in their own organizations. Overall, most respondents rated nearly all of the potential reasons for diversity to be at least somewhat important to their organizations. However, when they were asked to choose only one most important reason for workforce diversity in question 2, the largest group of managers (17%) surprisingly chose "Enhancing competitiveness," which was not even among the top six reasons in the answers to the previous question. The next largest group selected the reason, "It's the right thing to do," which positions diversity as a moral imperative rather than a business imperative. "Enlarging the pool of management talent" came in third. (A more detailed analysis of the reasons for diversity efforts appears in Schreiber, Price, & Morrison, 1994.)

If the top three responses for question 2 are somewhat surprising, the reasons at the bottom are even more so. The most important reasons for workforce diversity chosen least often by survey respondents are: "Reducing costs" (1%) and "Reducing employee turnover" (1%). Interestingly, these are the two business reasons most directly linked to diversity efforts, yet there is an obvious lack of importance given to them in the responses. That is, cost reductions, such as reduced turnover and absenteeism, are often documented as immediate and important benefits of diversity activities, some of the few tangible benefits that can be measured and relayed to top management (Caudron, 1990; Cox, 1993; Hymowitz, 1990; Stuart, 1992). Reducing costs and stemming the loss of talented employees are not only targeted outcomes of many diversity initiatives, but they are often the driving forces for the initiative itself. Corning, Inc., for example, a company known worldwide for its diversity efforts, began its substantial investment in diversity to reduce turnover (Morrison, Ruderman, & Hughes-James, 1993).

It seems unlikely that the 304 participants in our study discount these key reasons because they aren't as relevant in their organizations. Reducing costs and retaining talented workers are explicit priorities of many businesses and public-sector organizations. Instead these managers may not be as aware of the potential impact of diversity on these outcomes, perhaps because many haven't yet taken significant steps to address diversity issues.

Another surprise in question 2 is the lack of importance attributed to the practice of "Enlarging the pool of executive talent." Only 2% of the managers surveyed rated this the most important reason. Yet we saw earlier, in question 1, this was rated as one of the top reasons that diversity is important by this same group of respondents.

Some of these unexpected responses may occur because respondents are selecting as the most important reason outcomes that have long-term rather than short-term impact. Issues of cost reduction, for example, may lose significance when compared with the long-range competitiveness of an organization. However, the survey results as a whole suggest that a number of these managers don't see a strong connection between diversity and the health of their business, and because of this, may not support diversity issues to the extent that they are given priority over other business pressures. In contrast, many of the managers interviewed for the GOLD Project were explicit about how diversity would improve their organization's performance, both in the short- and long-term.

How Effective Are Organizations in Achieving Diversity?

The human resources managers surveyed in this study rate their organizations as effective in achieving diversity but only to a point. Half of the respondents indicated that their organizations have been either very effective or largely effective in achieving diversity in their entire workforce. Another 35% rate their organizations as being somewhat effective.

That success, however, doesn't carry into the management or executive ranks. Quite the contrary, most respondents consider their organizations to be less effective at progressively higher levels. Nearly half of the respondents, for example, rate their organizations ineffective or only slightly effective at the management level. And fully half of the respondents claim that their organizations are ineffective in achieving diversity at the executive level.

The ratings of managers in our survey are not unlike those of the managers in the Hay Group survey (Rigdon, 1992) where 55% rated themselves "average" on managing diversity; only 5% said they were doing a "very good" job, perhaps because diversity is still not evident in the management ranks of many organizations.

These responses correspond with statistics regularly published, which show that the majority of the workforce in the U.S. consists of nontraditional workers but that representation of nontraditionals drops off dramatically at higher management levels. In 1990 only 2.6% of the Fortune 500 companies' corporate officers were women, and commonly cited sources show that only 3 to 5% of senior executives, and less than 10% of all executives, are people of color or white women despite their significant presence in the workforce (The Feminist Majority Foundation, 1991; Galen & Palmer, 1994; Garland, 1991; Morrison & Von Glinow, 1990). The discrepancy between the growing diversity within the general workforce and the lagging integration at management levels shows that the glass ceiling continues to exist in most organizations.

As a group, the organizations surveyed seem to fall into the "average" category with respect to developing diversity, judging from respondents' self-ratings. We had hoped to collect some statistical data from these managers about the representation of nontraditionals at different levels within their organizations (see question 11), but the responses were too inconsistent to consider. Apparently, few organizations categorize employment data this way, so we were not able to get personnel profiles to match with self-ratings of effectiveness.

We did, however, separate the responses of those who rated their organizations as being at least somewhat effective (somewhat, largely, and very effective) and compared them with the other managers' responses with respect to the specific practices used in their organizations. This comparison suggests which practices are associated with greater reported success in achieving diversity, especially at the management and executive levels. Success at these levels, where the glass ceiling exists, is far more elusive than at the general workforce level.

Top Barriers to Advancement

The eighteen barriers in question 5 were derived from the twenty-one barriers in the GOLD Project. The glass ceiling is generally thought of as a combination of different factors that limit upward mobility for nontraditional managers. The types of barriers identified in this investigation and other recent studies include those at the organizational level—even society as a whole—as well as those at the individual and group levels. For example, prejudice was the top barrier identified by managers in the GOLD Project. Other studies identified similar barriers, such as racism and negative stereotypes, as major obstacles for people of color and white women in particular (Baskerville & Tucker, 1991; Catalyst, 1991; Morrison, White, & Van Velsor, 1992). These obstacles take form at the individual level, as well as at the group and organizational levels. Employees may offend co-workers by telling racist jokes, managers may make assumptions about the leadership potential of women, and organizations' recruitment policies may favor individuals most like those doing the hiring.

Periodically examining advancement barriers is important to determine which may need immediate attention. Like almost everything else, barriers are likely to change over time, and what was seen as most critical just a couple of years ago may not be judged so important today. Having current information about barriers lessens the possibility that managers will create solutions in search of problems—that is, adopt practices aimed at solving marginal problems rather than pursuing the root causes and addressing them.

The responses highlight specific elements of the glass ceiling that these human resources managers believe to be most pervasive, or most commonly encountered by nontraditional managers, in their organizations. Two of these eighteen barriers are most significant; they were rated as existing to a great extent by more than one-third of the managers surveyed: Traditional managers "have greater comfort with their own kind," and "Lack of accountability or incentives for developing diversity." Both were seen as existing at least to a moderate extent by about two-thirds of the respondents, regardless of the type of organization, more than any other barriers.

Only two other barriers came close: "Business restrictions" (such as downsizing) and "Inertia" (or a risk-averse culture that is slow to change). Nearly half of the survey respondents noted that these exist to a great or moderate extent. In fact, in a subsequent question about opportunities for promotion within the management ranks (question 7), most managers indicated that these opportunities declined at least somewhat in their organizations during the past five years. The recent economic recession and the prevalence of downsizing clearly constitute a barrier for many organizations. For some, the economic straitjacket may be contributing to a tendency to avoid risk-taking and do business in the traditional way.

Survey responses also indicate what these managers do *not* consider to be barriers in their organizations. More than three-fourths of the respondents noted that "Pay differentials" either do not exist as potential barriers or that they exist only to a slight extent. Nearly three-fourths of the managers ruled out two other barriers as well: Finding qualified women and people of color because they "have difficulty in balancing career and family," and women and people of color "are unwilling to relocate." Also, sixty percent of the respondents indicated that "Lack organizational savvy" is a nonexistent or slight barrier. Other potential barriers dismissed by most survey respondents include: "Conflicts between work and family"; an "Unsupportive, unfriendly work environment"; and "Isolating community environment."

Comparison to GOLD Project. Managers' perception of advancement barriers in this survey differ dramatically from the perceptions of managers interviewed for the GOLD Project (see Table 2). The latter group was asked to volunteer any barriers they believed affected people of color or white women in management. Of all the types of barriers they mentioned, six came up most frequently and account for fully half of all those mentioned.

The two groups of managers were asked essentially the same questions but show little agreement. Only one barrier appears on both lists of the most significant barriers—"greater comfort with their own kind." More than half of the 304 survey respondents also agreed that two others on the list of the top six barriers from the GOLD Project were a barrier in their organizations, at least to a small extent: "Inadequate or misguided career management" and traditional managers "are threatened by people who are different."

The remaining three of the top six barriers from the GOLD Project, however, were only infrequently rated as a problem by survey respondents. The managers surveyed more often rated a number of other barriers as a problem in their organization, including ineffective recruiting efforts, "Vague selection or promotion practices," and the tendency of white male managers

Table 2

Top Six Barriers Found in GOLD Project Research and the Glass Ceiling Benchmark Survey

Barriers

GOLD Project (N = 197) 21 Barriers	*Glass Ceiling Benchmark Survey* (N = 304) 18 Barriers
White men already in place, keep others out because of prejudice.	White men already in place, keep others out because they have greater comfort with their own kind.
White men already in place, keep others out because of other reasons (could not be further classified).	Lack of accountability or incentives for developing diversity.
Poor work environment.	Business reactions (such as downsizing).
Cannot find qualified nontraditional candidates because they lack organizational savvy.	Inertia, risk-averse culture.
White men already in place, keep others out because of greater comfort with their own kind.	Inadequate or misguided career management.
Cannot find qualified nontraditional candidates because they have difficulty balancing career and family life.	They are threatened by people who are different.

to be "insensitive or patronizing." (A more detailed discussion of our survey findings on diversity barriers can be found in the article by Schreiber et al., 1994.)

Differences in top barriers. Why are these two lists of top barriers so different? Is it possible that the top barriers in the 304 organizations in the Glass Ceiling Benchmark Survey are significantly different from those in the sixteen model organizations described in the GOLD Project? This seems unlikely since the barriers in the progressive organizations are very basic. Prejudice, for example, and an unsupportive, unfriendly work environment for nontraditional managers are not particularly sophisticated problems. One could reasonably expect these same problems to occur in most organizations, including ones that are not as experienced in developing diversity.

There are two more probable explanations for the different lists. One has to do with the methods used and the other concerns the level of expertise of the managers participating in the two studies. It is possible that the use of different methods in these two studies is partly responsible for the different results. It may be, for example, that the wording of some survey items was interpreted differently among respondents and prompted different responses. The GOLD Project interview allowed managers to describe barriers in their own words—classification into categories came later. The human resources managers were then given those categories on the survey.

One challenge with survey research is finding terms that are clear and descriptive so that they mean the same thing to all respondents. We made a concerted effort to do this and to avoid potentially inflammatory terms that might prompt an emotional response rather than an objective response. The word *prejudice,* for example, was not used in the survey (see item a.2 of question 5 in the Appendix), even though some of the managers interviewed used it; we recognized this as an emotionally charged word. Though we made a thorough effort, there's no guarantee that all the items meant exactly the same thing to every manager. That is a risk inherent in survey methodology. However, we believe that these method issues aren't the principal cause of differences in the responses.

A more likely explanation is that the differences are due to the level of knowledge and experience of the managers themselves. The managers interviewed for the GOLD Project, from organizations on the cutting edge of diversity within their own industry or sector, may have had more insight into barriers that exist because of their greater experience or success in reducing them. Work-family conflicts, for example, were downplayed as a barrier by survey respondents. Perhaps this issue is not a central one in many organiza-

Results and Discussion

tions. Or perhaps some of the surveyed managers fail to realize how serious these problems are for employees, possibly assuming that recently instituted policies and benefits in their organizations are more effective than they really are.

We can't say for certain why survey respondents rated potential barriers the way they did. There are hints, however, that survey respondents as a group, because of inexperience with diversity issues, may have less knowledge about and less commitment to them than managers interviewed for the GOLD Project. For example, their responses concerning the importance of diversity to their organizations, discussed in the "Key Practices" section below, suggest a credibility gap that may be adding to the difficulty of effectively confronting the glass ceiling. That is, many of these managers don't seem to view diversity as a legitimate business issue with bottom-line benefits. Such a gap may represent a major difference between the organizations surveyed and those selected as model organizations in the GOLD Project.

Summary. The 304 managers we surveyed gave support to the notion that the glass ceiling involves a variety of barriers that continue to exist in their organizations to at least some extent. Overall, barriers that these managers rated as most significant are quite different from the top barriers identified by managers in leading-edge organizations participating in the GOLD Project.

Use of different data-collection tools in the two studies may explain some of these differences. Some key differences appear to be due to the levels of knowledge and experience that the two groups of respondents have in the diversity arena. The surveyed group of managers may not yet be as advanced in identifying diversity problems and applying remedies as the group of managers originally interviewed for the GOLD Project. Their perceptions, therefore, as individuals or as members of organizations inexperienced in these matters, may be vaguer.

The managers in our survey clearly see two barriers—the discomfort factor and the lack of accountability—as the most serious in their organizations and as key elements of today's glass ceiling. It turns out that both of these barriers are also strongly related to their organizations' lack of success in developing diversity within the management and executive ranks. In other words, managers who rate their organizations as less effective at achieving diversity at these levels also indicate that discomfort and the lack of accountability are more prevalent.

The association between overall success and these two barriers suggests that they warrant special attention. We explore this relationship below and discuss how certain practices may be related to each of these key barriers and to the overall success of organizations in developing diversity at executive and management levels.

Key Practices

A total of fifty-two types of diversity practices emerged from the GOLD Project research. Of these, the ten practices identified as most important are shown in Table 3 with percentages of their importance in the Glass Ceiling Benchmark Survey as well as the rate of their implementation.

Table 3

Importance and Implementation in the Glass Ceiling Benchmark Survey of the Top Ten Diversity Practices from the GOLD Project

GOLD PROJECT	GLASS CEILING BENCHMARK SURVEY	
	% important and somewhat important*	% implemented[†]
1. Top management personally intervenes to encourage and reward managers to pursue diversity goals	72	26
2. Organization conducts targeted recruiting of women and people of color for nonmanagerial positions	79	50
3. Top management publicly and repeatedly advocates diversity both inside and outside the organization	48	16
4. There is an emphasis on EEO statistics, profiles	65	47
5. Progress on meeting diversity goals is included in managers' goals and performance evaluation	68	20
6. Diversity considerations are included in promotion criteria and decisions	72	20
7. Diversity considerations are included in management succession planning	74	22
8. Organization provides diversity training programs	75	29
9. Networks and support groups are active	76	18
10. Organization has work and family policies	86	38

$N = 197$

*See question 4, (1) [pp. 36-37].
[†]See question 4, (2) [pp. 38-39].

Results and Discussion 17

This list provides a point of comparison. We wanted to know which of these practices are most important in the 304 organizations in this survey and to what extent they are used. After this general backdrop, we focus on the practices that seem to be most closely linked to greater effectiveness in developing diversity.

The most prevalent diversity practices. Managers were asked to rate the thirty-nine practices in the Glass Ceiling Benchmark Survey in terms of their importance, their implementation status in the organization, and the effectiveness of the practices that had been implemented.

Seven practices were reported to be fully implemented by at least half of the respondents (see Table 4). Of these seven, the top three were also rated important by more than half of the respondents. These three were also rated largely effective or very effective by most respondents. For the remaining four, at least 40% of the respondents rated them important. Internship programs were also seen as especially effective by respondents—56% rated them largely or very effective.

Table 4

Most Prevalent Diversity Practices in the Glass Ceiling Benchmark Survey

Practice	% organizations fully implemented	% rated important	% rated largely or very effective
1. Organization has policies against racism, sexism	85	83	57
2. Organization has grievance procedures or complaint resolution process	76	68	58
3. Organization sponsors access to external training and seminars	69	49	48
4. Organization has active AA/EEO Committee/Office	61	39	30
5. Organization supports an internship program	53	44	56
6. Organization conducts internal audits or employee attitude surveys	50	47	42
7. Organization has partnerships with educational institutions (e.g., high schools, college teachers)	50	50	55

Few practices were consistently rated unimportant or only somewhat important. In fact, only two practices were rated less than somewhat important by most respondents—"Achieving diversity goals is recognized through events and awards" and "Internal advocacy groups are active." Regarding the status of implementation, several practices were rated as "not addressed" in most of the organizations surveyed. (That is, these practices weren't even being considered, let alone developed or implemented, in most of these organizations.) As to the effectiveness of practices, most respondents reported all of the practices to be at least somewhat effective.

Overall, there seems to be a tendency among respondents to rate practices that have already been implemented in their organizations as more important and more effective than other practices. The reverse is also true. Such responses are understandable; one would expect managers to see the good in the investments they have made (according to cognitive dissonance theory). In this case, some practices may come under the personal direction of the human resources managers who responded, and these managers may view them in a particularly positive light.

Very few practices had been tried and abandoned in these organizations. On the contrary, many different types of practices appear to be in the process of being evaluated or developed. It seems that diversity initiatives may be just getting underway. With the exception of only a few practices, many activities designed to foster diversity are still in the development pipeline.

The most critical diversity practices. The above discussion of practices that are most and least prevalent in this broad array of organizations provides an interesting context for current diversity activities. It does not, however, indicate which practices might be more important for organizations such as these to adopt. Popularity and importance do not necessarily go hand-in-hand.

The issue of importance should be specifically addressed, so managers can give priority to some practices over others. Because this survey queried human resources managers about (1) the importance of diversity practices and (2) the effectiveness of diversity practices that had been fully implemented, we are able to examine the perceived impact of these practices. We went further in our analysis, however, to address several compelling questions:

- Which practices are most closely associated with the presence or absence of the two key diversity barriers discussed earlier—lack of accountability and discomfort with nontraditionals?
- Which practices are most strongly related to an organization's effectiveness in achieving leadership diversity?

Results and Discussion

- What is the most important diversity practice?

Practices associated with the two key diversity barriers. We noted above that the two most significant barriers identified by the managers surveyed were the fact that traditional managers "have greater comfort with their own kind" and the "Lack of accountability or incentives for developing diversity." It is possible that certain practices are more effective at reducing these particularly troublesome barriers. If we can begin to identify these practices, then managers would have a basis for investing more in these practices over others.

Analysis of the survey responses showed that indeed some practices seem to be most closely related to these two key barriers. That is, certain practices are much more prevalent in organizations in which these barriers exist to a lesser extent than in other organizations. Statistically significant results demonstrate this relationship, not simply the managers' ratings themselves, as the following sections describe. Therefore, these practices may be ones to which managers should pay particular attention.

Lower "discomfort" barrier. In those organizations where white male managers' "greater comfort with their own kind" is seen as less of a barrier to nontraditional managers, the practices more often implemented are shown in Table 5. Each of these practices is strongly associated with a lower discomfort barrier; the correlations are all at the .005 level of statistical significance.

These five practices are very important, since they are statistically most closely related to the lower discomfort barrier in these organizations. The human resources managers we surveyed in these organizations, however, don't consider most of these practices to be very important. Only one of these five practices, "Organization has policies against racism, sexism," was seen as important by more than half of the managers surveyed. Three of the five, in contrast, were rated important by only about a quarter of the respondents.

Perhaps because these managers' perceptions don't match the statistical results, few of the practices that are most closely tied (statistically) to the lower discomfort barrier have been implemented in these organizations. Of these five practices, only one—"Organization has policies against racism, sexism"—has been fully implemented in the majority of these organizations. Two of them, the "Entry-level development program" and the "Networks and support groups," were reportedly used in less than 20% of the organizations surveyed. In other words, what seem to be the most promising solutions to a key barrier have not even been tried in most of these organizations.

Table 5

Diversity Practices Associated with Lower "Discomfort" Barrier

Practice	% rated important	Correlation with "Discomfort" Barrier	% fully implemented
1. Organization has liberal, progressive or benevolent image	26	-.31**	27
2. Organization has policies against racism, sexism	83	-.30**	85
3. There is an emphasis on EEO statistics, profiles	26	-.30**	47
4. Networks and support groups are active	25	-.29**	18
5. Entry-level development program exists for identified high-potential employees	34	-.23**	19

**$p < .005$

In the GOLD Project organizations, more of these practices were used. Two of the five practices were in the list of the top-ten best practices, used by more than half of the sixteen organizations: "emphasis on EEO statistics, profiles," and "Networks and support groups are active." A third, "Organization has policies against racism, sexism," was also used in more than half of the sixteen organizations. The other two practices were used in at least one-fourth of these organizations.

Combating the problem of discomfort is an intimidating task, and it seems to require a variety of types of practices to make progress. Understandably, many managers are unclear about how to attack this barrier, and they may adopt an array of different practices to reduce employees' discomfort. Some practices, such as employee networks, seem to be geared toward short-term comfort, particularly of nontraditionals. Providing more opportunities for black employees, employees with disabilities, single parents, and so forth to spend time with others with similar demographics and concerns may encourage them to stay. These networks also typically provide support and resources to address members' concerns. Entry-level development programs can also reduce discomfort with those who are different by including employees of different races, both sexes, various lifestyles, and so forth. These employees, all new to the organization, learn about one another as they learn

Results and Discussion

about the organization. They share one another's newness to the organization, which may make it easier for them to be comfortable with demographic differences; that greater comfort may last far into their careers.

Other practices appear to be geared more specifically to long-term comfort, even though they may lead to more discomfort in the short run. The emphasis on EEO profiles, for example, can be distressing to employees who want integration to evolve more naturally. However, these periodic "head counts" ensure that change in the composition of key groups of employees does, in fact, change from year to year by providing incentives for managers to pay attention to the demographic mix of their employees. It seems artificial to some employees, but others argue that such deliberate integration fosters working relationships that become more comfortable over time. Once employees who are different begin to work together, particularly as peers, their negative stereotypes about "those people" weaken because they get to know them personally, as individuals. The short-term awkwardness and even resentment by some employees may be a small price to pay for the potential comfort of all employees over the long term.

In organizations that have been struggling over the years to develop diversity in management, it may be more obvious that the required set of practices is complex and somewhat confrontational. Policies may look good and may be an important early step in confronting discomfort, but they don't stand on their own. Our results indicate that more of the practices most closely associated with a lower level of discomfort in the surveyed organizations have been implemented and are more valued in the leading-edge organizations that participated in the GOLD Project.

Lower "lack of accountability" barrier. For organizations in which accountability is seen as less of a barrier than in other organizations, which practices are most often used? The five practices most closely associated with a lower "lack of accountability" barrier in organizations are shown in Table 6. These five practices are very strongly statistically related to a lower "lack of accountability" barrier; the statistical significance is beyond the .001 level in each case. Further, all five of these practices were rated important by at least 40% of the managers surveyed. As we noted above, "Organization has policies against racism, sexism" was rated as particularly important, and an overwhelming majority of these managers (85%) reported that such policies have been fully implemented in their organizations.

However, there is still a substantial gap between what these managers believe to be important for diversity and what gets done in their organizations. The other four practices, despite their perceived importance, were only

Table 6

Diversity Practices Associated with Lower "Lack of Accountability" Barrier

Practice	% rated important	Correlation with "Lack of Accountability" Barrier	% fully implemented
1. Progress on meeting diversity goals is included in managers' goals and performance evaluation	45	-.51*	20
2. Top management personally intervenes to encourage and reward managers to pursue diversity goals	41	-.40*	12
3. Organization has policies against racism, sexism	83	-.38*	85
4. Organization conducts targeted recruiting of women and people of color for nonmanagerial positions	49	-.38*	50
5. Top management publicly and repeatedly advocates diversity both inside and outside the organization	50	-.37*	25

*$p < .01$

infrequently implemented. Less than a third of the respondents said their organizations had implemented *any* of these practices. In fact, the two practices with the highest statistical correlation are the least frequently used of these practices—"Top management personally intervenes to encourage and reward managers" (reported as fully implemented in only 12% of the participating organizations), and "Progress on meeting diversity goals is included in managers' goals and performance evaluation" (fully implemented in only 20% of these organizations).

Most of these five practices were far more dominant in the GOLD Project. The top management activities of encouraging, rewarding, and advocating for diversity (which were combined in the GOLD Project into one category called "personal intervention") were ranked at the top of the list, used by all sixteen organizations. Including diversity in performance evaluation and having policies against sexism and racism were used by the majority of these organizations. The practice of including diversity in selection criteria and decisions was far less prevalent in the GOLD Project. In that study, "selection" was treated as a leftover category, separate from recruitment, promotion, and succession-planning criteria and decision-making. Because the managers we surveyed may have treated some of these items as interchangeable in their responses, it is difficult to make comparisons about this practice.

Building accountability for diversity into organizations clearly requires action by top management and incorporating diversity goals into key organizational systems, such as how employees are chosen for jobs, evaluated, and rewarded. In the GOLD Project, some organizations changed their systems dramatically. They reexamined the criteria used to recruit or promote employees, for example, to see whether the traditional selection criteria were related at all to good performance. They comprised panels of managers to evaluate promotion candidates, so one manager's limited perspective wouldn't limit the choices. They quantified key diversity goals as best they could and wrote them into managers' performance expectations. All the while, senior executives repeated the diversity mandate in public and nagged behind the scenes to keep diversity goals at the top of employees' minds as they went about their work day after day.

The practices associated with this barrier don't overlap with those associated with the discomfort barrier, except for one—policies against racism and sexism. Perhaps this practice is so basic that it is required to form the foundation for a diversity initiative. The other eight practices found in Tables 5 and 6, however, may warrant special attention in confronting two very serious barriers that make up today's glass ceiling.

How do these eight practices compare with those that are most closely associated with overall effectiveness? The next section addresses that question.

Practices most closely associated with overall effectiveness. The previous two sections discussed practices that may be related to lowering certain barriers that were chosen by these managers as significant facets of the glass ceiling. Now we go beyond selected barriers to examine the relationship between the practices and the overall effectiveness in achieving diversity within the management and executive ranks of these 304 organizations. The managers surveyed were asked to rate their organization's effectiveness in achieving diversity in the workforce, in the management ranks, and in the executive ranks. We compared the responses of two groups: those who rated their organizations at least somewhat effective at the management and executive levels (the more effective group) and those who rated their organizations only slightly effective or ineffective at these levels (the less effective group). We then examined the practices used in these two groups. In terms of achieving diversity at these higher levels, the practices used in the organizations reported to be more effective should be more significant than practices used in organizations rated as less effective. Given all the types of diversity practices available to managers, it would be helpful to identify those that are most significant and could be most valuable in a diversity initiative aimed at the higher levels.

The practices most strongly associated with these organizations' effectiveness in achieving diversity at the management and executive levels are shown in Table 7. All five of these practices are in the administration category (the thirty-nine key practices on question 4 were divided into the following categories: management, policies/resources, administration, training and development, and recruiting and external relations) on the survey and have to do with holding managers accountable for developing diversity within the management ranks. This is consistent with the findings in the GOLD Project that, of the top-ten practices in these leading-edge organizations, seven concern accountability or enforcement of diversity-related objectives.

If you combine the two practices concerning management succession planning, then four of the top five effective practices in this survey (see Table 7) overlap with the most important practices identified in the GOLD Project (see Table 3). The one exception is the practice of "selection criteria and decisions include diversity considerations." However, as we noted earlier, there may be a semantics issue involved here. If in fact managers are using selection criteria and decisions to include practices used in the recruitment process, then all five of these practices overlap with those in the top-ten practices of the GOLD Project.

There is little overlap between the practices statistically associated with overall effectiveness and those associated with the two key barriers described above (only two practices). However, the same phenomenon concerning semantics again occurs: Most of these managers report that these practices are not particularly important in achieving diversity. That is, these managers don't see these practices to be nearly as important as the statistical correlations suggest, and they are only infrequently used in these organizations. Even when they are used, only about one-third of the managers rating them say they are effective. Instead, more managers rate other practices as effective, and those rated very effective or largely effective by the majority of managers are not statistically associated with effectiveness. These are: "Organization has grievance procedures or complaint resolution process" (58% of

Table 7

Diversity Practices Associated with Effectiveness at Management and Executive Levels

Practice	Correlation with Effectiveness Mgmt	Correlation with Effectiveness Exec	% rated important	% implemented fully	% implemented under way	% rated largely/ very effective
1. Progress in meeting diversity goals included in goals and performance evaluation	.59***	.43**	45	20	15	30
2. Diversity considerations included in promotion criteria and decisions	.56***	.39**	42	20	23	35
3. Diversity considerations included in management succession planning	.52**	.46***	48	22	20	35
4. Competence in managing a diverse workforce is considered in management succession planning	.49**	.49**	38	9	16	33
5. Selection criteria and decisions include diversity considerations	.47***	.31**	47	32	24	31

** $p < .005$
*** $p < .0005$

managers rated this effective), "Organization has policies against racism, sexism" (55%), "Organization supports an internship program" (56%), and "Organization has partnerships with educational institutions" (55%).

Why is it that managers seem to value practices different from those that are statistically most closely related to key outcomes? They may be basing their ratings on what they believe has worked in the general workforce rather than what is most effective at higher levels. These managers have experienced success mostly at the lower levels, judging from their responses to question 6, and they may be assuming that what works there will also work at higher levels. Since they haven't yet made much progress in developing diversity at the management and executive levels, they may rely too heavily on their track record at lower levels in making judgments about importance and effectiveness.

Basic employee policies and recruitment techniques may be critical components of a foundation for developing diversity in any organization, beginning at the lower rungs of the organization. They may prove to be related to effectiveness at these levels, but they don't seem to foster much progress at higher ones. Rather, quite different practices seem to be needed to make headway at the leadership levels, as Table 7 shows.

The most significant diversity practice. The most significant practice found in this survey—the one that is statistically most closely associated with effectiveness at the management and executive levels—is "Progress on meeting diversity goals is included in managers' goals and performance evaluation." This practice is strongly correlated with overall effectiveness, and it shows a strong correlation with a lower "lack of accountability" barrier (see Tables 6 and 7). Unfortunately, it is used in only 20% of the organizations surveyed and is not seen as particularly important by the human resources managers who responded.

Perhaps this practice is so important because performance-management tools are the first step in creating accountability for developing diversity. In the performance-appraisal process, goals are made explicit and concrete, and the results of managers' efforts to achieve these goals are officially recognized. Because performance appraisal feeds into many other administrative tools, such as compensation and promotions, it serves as the backbone of an accountability system. That is, performance goals and evaluation represent the starting point for a meaningful accountability system for managers.

This may be the reason that the practice of including progress on diversity in the performance-evaluation system was found to be so important in the GOLD Project. This practice ranked fifth in importance of all the fifty-two practices identified. The appraisal systems in these model organizations incorporate diversity goals in a variety of ways. In one company, for example, every manager is evaluated on four objectives, including diversity. Managers must show how their personnel profile changed from one period to another and which employees received the benefits of a training program.

In other organizations the performance-appraisal process helps bring diversity goals to the forefront and extends to managers' compensation. In one case, up to 25% of a manager's evaluation can hinge on achieving diversity goals. Although half of the evaluation is based on traditional business goals, 15 to 30% of the final rating hinge on meeting affirmative-action goals, and 20 to 35% involve training, development, and motivating employees.

As in other organizations, the emphasis here is not only on meeting numerical goals but also on creating an atmosphere where employees are more comfortable trying new things and preparing to move up. This company has also required managers to meet 90% of *all* their goals to receive *any* of their annual bonus. In another company, parity in management is only one small part of the basis for managers' bonuses, but managers who fail to meet affirmative-action goals can lose up to 10% of their total bonus.

Including diversity in the performance-appraisal process is a practice that can serve as the backbone of a system that sets performance expectations and helps determine consequences for meeting, or not meeting, those expectations. Explicitly including diversity in managers' (and other employees') expectations takes these goals from the back burner and ties them to the organization's long-term mission and business objectives.

Implications of key practices for organizations wishing to implement them. The results of this survey, in comparison with findings in the GOLD Project, indicate that quite a few organizations are indeed still newcomers to diversity, and that they haven't yet implemented the kinds of practices that are most likely to help them make progress at the management and executive levels.

The most promising diversity practice, one that should be considered as a keystone in any organization's diversity effort, is that of including progress on diversity in the performance-appraisal goals and ratings. Clearly, managers should give this practice priority as they pursue diversity in their organizations. Other promising practices worthy of consideration in any organization include the remaining four that were most closely correlated with overall effectiveness at the management and executive levels (see Table 7). These overlap considerably with the top-ten best practices identified in the GOLD Project (shown in Table 3).

Other practices that warrant managers' attention in addressing diversity issues at the leadership levels of organizations include those that were most strongly correlated with the lower barriers of discomfort and lack of accountability (shown in Tables 5 and 6), and the remaining practices on the top-ten list from the GOLD Project (shown in Table 3).

The most prevalent practices identified in this survey do not seem to represent the most promising solutions to the glass ceiling. They may or may not be effective in developing diversity at lower levels, but there are indications that they do not provoke meaningful change at higher levels.

Making decisions about which practices to adopt or emphasize is a key step in the process of developing diversity. There are, however, other steps that also need to be taken, which are likely to affect decisions about the practices themselves (Morrison & Crabtree, 1993). A critical first step is assessment, or (re)discovering the problems and strengths that now exist within the organization. Doing a thorough assessment before proceeding with the step of implementing practices helps ensure that employees are involved from the start, that their priorities are not overlooked, and that pockets of strength are used as a basis in constructing solutions. Assessment was identified as the first step in a five-step change process recommended for organizations to develop diversity at leadership levels (Morrison, 1992).

Assessment involves answering questions about the business impact of diversity, such as: Are we losing talented nontraditional (and traditional) managers? Do some groups of employees have more access to developmental opportunities or promotions than others? What is this turnover costing us? What are other costs that we might reduce (legal settlements, absenteeism, and so on)? What would help our employees be more productive? Establishing a baseline of information using records and interviews or focus groups helps determine which problems are most important and, as a result, which types of practices might be more urgently needed.

The assessment step also helps in constructing a strong business case for diversity, which appears to be desperately needed in many organizations. Managers should be able to detail potential benefits and cost savings as new practices are introduced. Changing managers' appraisal criteria, for example, requires an explanation of how the new criteria, and the goals concerning diversity in particular, will help accomplish the objectives for the organization and ultimately benefit everyone. No practice, not even the one we found in this study to be most important, can substitute for a level of understanding among employees about why the investment in diversity is being made.

Assessment also involves external benchmarking—examining other organizations' best practices—not unlike what we have done in this research. A common mistake in benchmarking, however, is to use the wrong organizations or the wrong methods to determine which practices to copy or adapt. As we saw in this survey, many organizations have not made much headway in developing diversity, and many managers don't yet have a good feel for which practices are most important or most effective. Making decisions based on the most prevalent practices found in this study could seriously mislead managers in their diversity efforts. External benchmarking needs to be done in a thoughtful, controlled way to be helpful. Internal benchmarking may be a much more useful approach for many organizations.

The results of an assessment form the foundation for creating a mix of practices that will help develop diversity in any given organization. Even so, some practices appear to be generally more promising than others, as our survey results indicate. These practices, especially that of including progress on diversity in the performance-evaluation process, should be high on the list for managers to consider when they reach this step.

References

Baskerville, D. M., & Tucker, S. H. (1991, November). A blueprint for success. *Black Enterprise*, pp. 85-93.

Catalyst. (1991). *Women in corporate management: Model programs for development and mobility.* New York: Catalyst.

Caudron, S. (1990, November). Monsanto responds to diversity. *Personnel Journal*, pp. 72-80.

Copeland, L. (1988, November). Valuing workplace diversity: Ten reasons employers recognize the benefits of a mixed workforce. *Personnel Administrator*, pp. 38, 40.

Cox, T. (1991, May). The multicultural organization. *Academy of Management Executive, 5*(2), 34-47.

Cox, T. (1993). *Cultural diversity in organizations: Theory, research, and practice* (1st ed.). San Francisco: Berrett-Koehler.

Feminist Majority Foundation. (1991). *Empowering women in business.* Washington, DC: Feminist Majority Foundation, p. 1.

Galen, M., & Palmer, A. T. (1994, January 31). White, male, and worried. *Business Week*, p. 52.

Garland, S. (1991, August 19). Throwing stones at the 'glass ceiling.' *Business Week*, p. 29.

Human Resource Planning Society/Center for Creative Leadership. (1992, November). *Glass Ceiling Survey: Report to participants.* New York: Authors.

Hymowitz, C. (1990, June 18). As Aetna adds flextime, bosses learn to cope. *The Wall Street Journal,* pp. B1-2.

Johnston, W. B., & Packer, A. H. (1987). *Workforce 2000: Work and workers for the 21st century.* Indianapolis: The Hudson Institute.

Morrison, A. M. (1992). *The new leaders: Guidelines on leadership diversity in America.* San Francisco: Jossey-Bass.

Morrison, A. M., & Crabtree, K. M. (1993). *Developing diversity in organizations: A digest of selected literature* (Report No. 317). Greensboro, NC: Center for Creative Leadership.

Morrison, A. M., Ruderman, M. N., & Hughes-James, M. (1993). *Making diversity happen: Controversies and solutions* (Report No. 320). Greensboro, NC: Center for Creative Leadership.

Morrison, A. M., & Von Glinow, M. (1990, February). Women and minorities in management. *American Psychologist,* p. 200.

Morrison, A. M., White, R. P., & Van Velsor, E. (1992). *Breaking the glass ceiling: Can women reach the top of America's largest corporations?* (2nd ed.). Reading, MA: Addison-Wesley.

Price, K. F., Schreiber, C. T., & Morrison, A. M. (1994). The "glass ceiling": Where we stand and what American business is doing about it. In C. Fay (Ed.), *Achieving organizational success: Through innovative human resource strategies* (Volume 1 of the Proceedings of the Fifth Human Resource Planning Society Research Symposium; pp. 159-175). New York: Human Resource Planning Society.

Rigdon, J. E. (1992, May 22). Managing. *The Wall Street Journal,* p. B-1.

Schreiber, C. T., Price, K. F., & Morrison, A. M. (1994, March). Workforce diversity and the glass ceiling: Practices, barriers, possibilities. *Human Resource Planning, 16*(2), 47-68.

Stuart, P. (1992, November). What does the glass ceiling cost you? *Personnel Journal,* pp. 70-80.

Training and Development. (1991, March). How big is the problem? p. 43.

U.S. Department of Labor. (1991). *A report on the glass ceiling initiative.* Washington, DC: U.S. Department of Labor.

Appendix

Survey Questions and Responses
(304 Respondents)

QUESTION #1

How important is a diverse workforce to your organization in terms of:

Percent Responding

		1 Unimportant	2 Somewhat unimportant	3 Neither important nor unimportant	4 Somewhat important	5 Important
a.	Increasing productivity	8	6	34	26	26
b.	Reducing costs	16	9	47	16	12
c.	Reducing employee turnover	10	5	25	40	20
d.	Increasing employee job satisfaction	6	4	14	45	31
e.	Facilitating recruiting	3	1	11	40	45
f.	Improving decision making	5	5	31	34	25
g.	Enhancing customer satisfaction	4	4	26	35	31
h.	Increasing creativity	7	3	21	37	32
i.	Enhancing competitiveness	5	3	22	34	36
j.	Enlarging pool of management talent	4	4	10	33	49
k.	Enlarging pool of executive talent	4	3	15	31	47
l.	Representing diversity of marketplace to which organization is trying to sell its products or services	7	7	16	29	41
m.	Representing the demographics of the community in which organization is located	4	5	12	37	42
n.	Meeting government regulations	5	3	16	38	38
o.	Avoiding affirmative action/equal opportunity issues	5	5	11	45	34
p.	"It's the right thing to do"	3	4	13	35	45
q.	Other (please specify)					

QUESTION #2

Of the reasons for workforce diversity listed in Question #1, which is **most important** to your organization?

		Percent Selecting *Most Important*
a.	Increasing productivity	5
b.	Reducing costs	1
c.	Reducing employee turnover	1
d.	Increasing employee job satisfaction	5
e.	Facilitating recruiting	5
f.	Improving decision making	2
g.	Enhancing customer satisfaction	4
h.	Increasing creativity	3
i.	Enhancing competitiveness	17
j.	Enlarging pool of management talent	11
k.	Enlarging pool of executive talent	2
l.	Representing diversity of marketplace to which organization is trying to sell its products or services	7
m.	Representing the demographics of the community in which organization is located	7
n.	Meeting government regulations	9
o.	Avoiding affirmative action/equal opportunity issues	8
p.	"It's the right thing to do"	13

QUESTION #3

Given all of the issues facing your organization, how important is the issue of workforce diversity?

		Percent
a.	Unimportant	3
b.	Somewhat unimportant	9
c.	Neither important nor unimportant	15
d.	Somewhat important	44
e.	Important	29

QUESTION #4

Listed below are a number of practices used by organizations to achieve diversity in their **executive and management** ranks. Please indicate, in terms of achieving diversity in your **executive and management** talent:

(1) HOW IMPORTANT EACH OF THESE PRACTICES ARE,
(2) the extent to which your organization is developing, implementing, or evaluating each of the following practices, and
(3) for those practices that are fully implemented, how effective have the practices been?

Percent Responding

Scale: 1 = Unimportant, 2 = Somewhat unimportant, 3 = Neither important nor unimportant, 4 = Somewhat important, 5 = Important

	MANAGEMENT	1	2	3	4	5
a.	Top management personally intervenes to encourage and reward managers to pursue diversity goals	9	6	13	31	41
b.	Top management provides resources to support workforce diversity (e.g., space, time, money)	9	7	11	29	44
c.	Top management publicly and repeatedly advocates diversity both inside and outside the organization	7	6	10	27	50
d.	Organization has an active AA/EEO Committee/Office	8	5	13	35	39
e.	Board of Directors demonstrates commitment to diversity through its composition	14	6	15	29	36
f.	Board of Directors' members demonstrate commitment to workforce diversity through their activities	16	6	20	27	31
g.	Other (please specify)					

	POLICIES/RESOURCES	1	2	3	4	5
a.	Organization has work and family policies	2	3	9	34	52
b.	Organization has policies against racism, sexism	0	1	2	14	83
c.	Organization has grievance procedures or complaint resolution process	1	1	6	24	68
d.	Child-care resources are available	9	3	17	37	34
e.	Personnel resources are available to help facilitate employee group meetings or other diversity activities	6	6	17	41	30
f.	Internal advocacy groups are active	15	11	26	28	20
g.	Networks and support groups are active	11	6	23	35	25
h.	Informal networking activities are taking place	5	6	13	38	38
i.	Organization uses a formal mentoring program	14	8	24	35	19
j.	Informal mentoring activities are taking place	5	3	13	38	41
k.	Other (please specify)					

Appendix

QUESTION #4 (continued)

Listed below are a number of practices used by organizations to achieve diversity in their **executive and management** ranks. Please indicate, in terms of achieving diversity in your **executive and management** talent:

(1) HOW IMPORTANT EACH OF THESE PRACTICES ARE,

Percent Responding

		Unimportant 1	Somewhat unimportant 2	Neither important nor unimportant 3	Somewhat important 4	Important 5
ADMINISTRATION						
a.	Progress on meeting diversity goals is included in managers' goals and performance evaluation	14	6	12	23	45
b.	Diversity considerations are included in promotion criteria and decisions	8	4	16	30	42
c.	Competence in managing a diverse workforce is considered in management succession planning	14	3	16	29	38
d.	Diversity considerations are included in management succession planning	9	3	14	26	48
e.	Progress on diversity goals is included in determining managers' compensation	17	7	17	29	30
f.	Selection criteria and decisions include diversity considerations	5	3	10	35	47
g.	Achieving diversity goals is recognized through events and awards	22	8	28	23	19
h.	There is an emphasis on EEO statistics, profiles	9	7	19	39	26
i.	Organization conducts internal audits or employee attitude surveys	6	5	10	32	47
j.	Other (please specify)					
TRAINING AND DEVELOPMENT						
a.	Organization provides diversity training programs	8	5	12	30	45
b.	Development programs exist for all high-potential managers	8	2	7	27	56
c.	Job rotations are encouraged for development	6	4	12	35	43
d.	Entry-level development program exists for identified high-potential employees	13	5	18	30	34
e.	Internal training programs exist for women and people of color	17	7	21	27	28
f.	Development programs exist specifically for women and people of color identified as having high potential	17	9	23	27	24
g.	Organization sponsors access to external training and seminars	3	1	8	39	49
h.	Other (please specify)					
RECRUITING AND EXTERNAL RELATIONS						
a.	Organization conducts targeted recruiting of women and people of color for nonmanagerial positions	8	3	10	30	49
b.	Key outside mid-career hires are used to enhance diversity	14	4	15	37	30
c.	Organization supports an internship program	8	4	18	26	44
d.	Organization's diversity efforts are given extensive public exposure	16	10	23	30	21
e.	Organization has liberal, progressive or benevolent image	12	5	26	31	26
f.	Organization has partnerships with educational institutions (e.g., high schools, technical schools, college teachers)	6	2	7	35	50
g.	Organization has partnerships with nontraditional groups (e.g., National Urban League, black or Hispanic MBA associations)	11	2	17	28	43
h.	Other (please specify)					

QUESTION #4 (continued)

Listed below are a number of practices used by organizations to achieve diversity in their **executive and management** ranks. Please indicate, in terms of achieving diversity in your **executive and management** talent:

(2) THE EXTENT TO WHICH YOUR ORGANIZATION IS DEVELOPING, IMPLEMENTING, OR EVALUATING EACH OF THE FOLLOWING PRACTICES,

Percent Responding

		1 Not addressed	2 Being evaluated	3 Under development	4 Implementation under way	5 Already fully implemented	6 Tried and abandoned
MANAGEMENT							
a.	Top management personally intervenes to encourage and reward managers to pursue diversity goals	24	17	20	26	12	1
b.	Top management provides resources to support workforce diversity (e.g., space, time, money)	25	11	17	32	15	0
c.	Top management publicly and repeatedly advocates diversity both inside and outside the organization	21	10	18	26	25	0
d.	Organization has an active AA/EEO Committee/Office	18	5	2	12	61	2
e.	Board of Directors demonstrates commitment to diversity through its composition	38	9	13	17	23	0
f.	Board of Directors' members demonstrate commitment to workforce diversity through their activities	49	9	13	13	16	0
g.	Other (please specify)						
POLICIES/RESOURCES							
a.	Organization has work and family policies	11	13	10	27	38	1
b.	Organization has policies against racism, sexism	2	1	0	9	85	3
c.	Organization has grievance procedures or complaint resolution process	5	3	3	12	76	1
d.	Child-care resources are available	29	17	8	12	32	2
e.	Personnel resources are available to help facilitate employee group meetings or other diversity activities	28	10	10	20	32	0
f.	Internal advocacy groups are active	52	9	9	13	16	1
g.	Networks and support groups are active	45	14	10	12	18	1
h.	Informal networking activities are taking place	25	7	9	26	32	1
i.	Organization uses a formal mentoring program	46	23	10	12	7	2
j.	Informal mentoring activities are taking place	27	12	10	22	28	1
k.	Other (please specify)						

Appendix

QUESTION #4 (continued)

Listed below are a number of practices used by organizations to achieve diversity in their **executive and management** ranks. Please indicate, in terms of achieving diversity in your **executive and management** talent:

(2) THE EXTENT TO WHICH YOUR ORGANIZATION IS DEVELOPING, IMPLEMENTING, OR EVALUATING EACH OF THE FOLLOWING PRACTICES,

Percent Responding

1. Not addressed
2. Being evaluated
3. Under development
4. Implementation under way
5. Already fully implemented
6. Tried and abandoned

ADMINISTRATION

		1	2	3	4	5	6
a.	Progress on meeting diversity goals is included in managers' goals and performance evaluation	35	13	16	15	20	1
b.	Diversity considerations are included in promotion criteria and decisions	32	11	14	23	20	0
c.	Competence in managing a diverse workforce is considered in management succession planning	43	17	15	16	9	0
d.	Diversity considerations are included in management succession planning	29	12	17	20	22	0
e.	Progress on diversity goals is included in determining managers' compensation	55	12	11	11	10	1
f.	Selection criteria and decisions include diversity considerations	17	13	14	24	32	0
g.	Achieving diversity goals is recognized through events and awards	71	9	7	4	9	0
h.	There is an emphasis on EEO statistics, profiles	21	7	7	16	47	2
i.	Organization conducts internal audits or employee attitude surveys	15	8	9	14	50	4
j.	Other (please specify)						

TRAINING AND DEVELOPMENT

		1	2	3	4	5	6
a.	Organization provides diversity training programs	20	14	16	19	29	2
b.	Development programs exist for all high-potential managers	21	12	16	18	32	1
c.	Job rotations are encouraged for development	22	15	15	19	29	0
d.	Entry-level development program exists for identified high-potential employees	43	18	8	11	19	1
e.	Internal training programs exist for women and people of color	51	12	9	6	21	1
f.	Development programs exist specifically for women and people of color identified as having high potential	62	14	6	7	10	1
g.	Organization sponsors access to external training and seminars	6	4	5	13	69	3
h.	Other (please specify)						

RECRUITING AND EXTERNAL RELATIONS

		1	2	3	4	5	6
a.	Organization conducts targeted recruiting of women and people of color for nonmanagerial positions	18	5	9	17	50	1
b.	Key outside mid-career hires are used to enhance diversity	39	9	9	16	26	1
c.	Organization supports an internship program	20	4	6	13	53	4
d.	Organization's diversity efforts are given extensive public exposure	51	11	9	12	16	1
e.	Organization has liberal, progressive or benevolent image	42	9	8	13	27	1
f.	Organization has partnerships with educational institutions (e.g., high schools, technical schools, college teachers)	13	2	10	22	50	3
g.	Organization has partnerships with nontraditional groups (e.g., National Urban League, black or Hispanic MBA associations)	26	7	9	13	43	2
h.	Other (please specify)						

QUESTION #4 (continued)

Listed below are a number of practices used by organizations to achieve diversity in their **executive and management** ranks. Please indicate, in terms of achieving diversity in your **executive and management** talent:

(3) FOR THOSE PRACTICES THAT ARE FULLY IMPLEMENTED, HOW EFFECTIVE HAVE THE PRACTICES BEEN?

Percent Responding

		Ineffective (1)	Somewhat ineffective (2)	Neither effective nor ineffective (3)	Largely effective (4)	Very effective (5)
MANAGEMENT						
a.	Top management personally intervenes to encourage and reward managers to pursue diversity goals	6	20	39	21	14
b.	Top management provides resources to support workforce diversity (e.g., space, time, money)	5	17	38	30	10
c.	Top management publicly and repeatedly advocates diversity both inside and outside the organization	5	22	34	26	13
d.	Organization has an active AA/EEO Committee/Office	4	17	49	23	7
e.	Board of Directors demonstrates commitment to diversity through its composition	14	20	23	27	16
f.	Board of Directors' members demonstrate commitment to workforce diversity through their activities	12	24	34	20	10
g.	Other (please specify)					
POLICIES/RESOURCES						
a.	Organization has work and family policies	4	7	45	31	13
b.	Organization has policies against racism, sexism	2	9	34	43	12
c.	Organization has grievance procedures or complaint resolution process	2	13	27	43	15
d.	Child-care resources are available	9	18	30	26	17
e.	Personnel resources are available to help facilitate employee group meetings or other diversity activities	5	16	35	34	10
f.	Internal advocacy groups are active	18	14	35	18	15
g.	Networks and support groups are active	10	19	38	23	10
h.	Informal networking activities are taking place	5	18	42	26	9
i.	Organization uses a formal mentoring program	19	26	32	17	6
j.	Informal mentoring activities are taking place	4	19	39	29	9
k.	Other (please specify)					

Appendix

QUESTION #4 (continued)

Listed below are a number of practices used by organizations to achieve diversity in their **executive and management** ranks. Please indicate, in terms of achieving diversity in your **executive and management** talent:

(3) FOR THOSE PRACTICES THAT ARE FULLY IMPLEMENTED, HOW EFFECTIVE HAVE THE PRACTICES BEEN?

Percent Responding

		Ineffective (1)	Somewhat ineffective (2)	Neither effective nor ineffective (3)	Largely effective (4)	Very effective (5)
ADMINISTRATION						
a.	Progress on meeting diversity goals is included in managers' goals and performance evaluation	13	20	37	18	12
b.	Diversity considerations are included in promotion criteria and decisions	10	18	37	25	10
c.	Competence in managing a diverse workforce is considered in management succession planning	14	18	35	22	11
d.	Diversity considerations are included in management succession planning	7	23	35	27	8
e.	Progress on diversity goals is included in determining managers' compensation	23	15	30	17	15
f.	Selection criteria and decisions include diversity considerations	4	19	46	25	6
g.	Achieving diversity goals is recognized through events and awards	23	23	21	18	15
h.	There is an emphasis on EEO statistics, profiles	7	29	40	21	3
i.	Organization conducts internal audits or employee attitude surveys	6	14	38	30	12
j.	Other (please specify)					
TRAINING AND DEVELOPMENT						
a.	Organization provides diversity training programs	4	15	44	24	13
b.	Development programs exist for all high-potential managers	6	10	35	35	14
c.	Job rotations are encouraged for development	7	15	36	32	10
d.	Entry-level development program exists for identified high-potential employees	11	15	33	31	10
e.	Internal training programs exist for women and people of color	15	14	28	29	14
f.	Development programs exist specifically for women and people of color identified as having high potential	21	17	27	22	13
g.	Organization sponsors access to external training and seminars	2	10	40	37	11
h.	Other (please specify)					
RECRUITING AND EXTERNAL RELATIONS						
a.	Organization conducts targeted recruiting of women and people of color for nonmanagerial positions	2	10	41	33	14
b.	Key outside mid-career hires are used to enhance diversity	9	12	20	21	18
c.	Organization supports an internship program	2	12	30	35	21
d.	Organization's diversity efforts are given extensive public exposure	9	18	34	26	13
e.	Organization has liberal, progressive or benevolent image	10	17	31	27	15
f.	Organization has partnerships with educational institutions (e.g., high schools, technical schools, college teachers)	3	12	30	34	21
g.	Organization has partnerships with nontraditional groups (e.g., National Urban League, black or Hispanic MBA associations)	7	12	36	24	21
h.	Other (please specify)					

QUESTION #5

To what extent do each of the following barriers to achieving diversity **currently exist** in your **executive and managerial** ranks?

Percent Responding

1 = Does not exist
2 = Exists to a slight extent
3 = Exists to a small extent
4 = Exists to a moderate extent
5 = Exists to a great extent

		1	2	3	4	5
a.	Traditional managers (white males) are already in place, limiting access to women and people of color because:					
	1. They have greater comfort with their own kind	6	9	13	35	37
	2. They see difference as a deficiency	22	22	24	24	8
	3. They are threatened by people who are different	18	25	23	22	12
	4. They are insensitive or patronizing	22	21	21	25	11
b.	Cannot find qualified candidates who are women or people of color because they:					
	1. Lack required education	31	25	19	19	6
	2. Lack organizational savvy	37	22	20	15	6
	3. Are unwilling to relocate	45	26	12	11	6
	4. Have difficulty in balancing career and family	45	28	17	10	0
c.	Cannot find qualified candidates who are women or people of color because of ineffective recruiting efforts	21	18	25	26	10
d.	Vague selection or promotion practices	26	20	18	25	11
e.	Inadequate or misguided career management	17	22	24	23	14
f.	Unsupportive, unfriendly work environment	33	26	19	16	6
g.	Isolating community environment	38	20	15	18	9
h.	Conflicts between work and family	29	36	20	13	2
i.	Lack of accountability or incentives for developing diversity	11	12	15	27	35
j.	Business restrictions (such as downsizing)	22	16	15	24	23
k.	Inertia, risk averse culture	14	20	20	26	20
l.	Pay differentials	59	18	13	6	4
m.	Other (please specify)					

Appendix

QUESTION #6

Overall, how effective has your organization been in achieving diversity in your workforce? Management ranks? Executive ranks?

		Ineffective 1	Slightly effective 2	Somewhat effective 3	Largely effective 4	Very effective 5
a.	Workforce	4	11	35	34	16
b.	Management	13	35	39	10	3
c.	Executive	49	31	13	3	4

QUESTION #7

During the past five years, how has the opportunity for promotions changed within your organization's management ranks?

		Percent
a.	Declined significantly	19
b.	Declined somewhat	32
c.	Stayed about the same	23
d.	Increased somewhat	18
e.	Increased significantly	8

QUESTION #8

DEMOGRAPHICS
Industry

		Number	Percent
a.	Not classified	4	1
b.	Agriculture	1	0
c.	Manufacturing, all other	40	13
d.	Chemicals and allied products	10	3
e.	Communications equipment	3	1
f.	Communications services	8	3
g.	Construction	4	1
h.	Consumer products	21	7
i.	Diversified	9	3
j.	Drugs and pharmaceuticals	10	3
k.	Education	13	4
l.	Electrical & electronic equipment	16	5
m.	Financial institutions	30	10
n.	Health services	19	6
o.	Insurance	20	7
p.	Other not-for-profit	11	4
q.	Petroleum, mining & related products	5	2
r.	Printing and publishing	7	2
s.	Public sector (government)	14	5
t.	Real estate	0	0
u.	Retail and wholesale	8	3
v.	Services	15	5
w.	Transportation	6	2
x.	Utilities	21	7
y.	Wood, paper and packaging	7	2

Appendix   45

QUESTION #9

Organizational unit

		Number	Percent
a.	Total organization	236	80
b.	Division or other unit	60	20

QUESTION #10

Number of employees in unit described in Question 9

a.	Less than 1,000	54	18
b.	1,000 to 4,999	81	27
c.	5,000 to 9,999	44	15
d.	10,000 to 25,000	50	17
e.	More than 25,000	70	23

QUESTION #11

Employment distribution for unit described in Question 9*

Percent of employees	White		People of Color	
	Male	Female	Male	Female
a. All employees	___%	___%	___%	___%
b. Managers	___%	___%	___%	___%
c. Executives	___%	___%	___%	___%

*Responses are not shown because the format of this question was apparently confusing and led to inconsistencies and non-comparability among respondents.

CENTER FOR CREATIVE LEADERSHIP PUBLICATIONS

SELECTED REPORTS:

Beyond Work-Family Programs J.R. Kofodimos (1995, Stock #167) $25.00
CEO Selection: A Street-Smart Review G.P. Hollenbeck (1994, Stock #164) $25.00
Coping With an Intolerable Boss M.M. Lombardo & M.W. McCall, Jr. (1984, Stock #305) $10.00
The Creative Opportunists: Conversations with the CEOs of Small Businesses
J.S. Bruce (1992, Stock #316) $12.00
Creativity in the R&D Laboratory T.M. Amabile & S.S. Gryskiewicz (1987, Stock #130)............... $12.00
Eighty-eight Assignments for Development in Place: Enhancing the Developmental
Challenge of Existing Jobs M.M. Lombardo & R.W. Eichinger (1989, Stock #136) $15.00
Enhancing 360-degree Feedback for Senior Executives: How to Maximize the Benefits and
Minimize the Risks R.E. Kaplan & C.J. Palus (1994, Stock #160) $15.00
An Evaluation of the Outcomes of a Leadership Development Program C.D. McCauley &
M.W. Hughes-James (1994, Stock #163) $35.00
Evolving Leaders: A Model for Promoting Leadership Development in Programs C.J. Palus &
W.H. Drath (1995, Stock #165) $20.00
Feedback to Managers, Volume I: A Guide to Evaluating Multi-rater Feedback Instruments
E. Van Velsor & J. Brittain Leslie (1991, Stock #149) $20.00
Feedback to Managers, Volume II: A Review and Comparison of Sixteen Multi-rater
Feedback Instruments E. Van Velsor & J. Brittain Leslie (1991, Stock #150) $80.00
Gender Differences in the Development of Managers: How Women Managers Learn From
Experience E. Van Velsor & M. W. Hughes (1990, Stock #145) $35.00
A Glass Ceiling Survey: Benchmarking Barriers and Practices A.M. Morrison, C.T. Schreiber,
& K.F. Price (1995, Stock #161) $20.00
High Hurdles: The Challenge of Executive Self-Development R.E. Kaplan, W.H. Drath, &
J.R. Kofodimos (1985, Stock #125) $15.00
The Intuitive Pragmatists: Conversations with Chief Executive Officers J.S. Bruce
(1986, Stock #310) $12.00
Key Events in Executives' Lives E.H. Lindsey, V. Homes, & M.W. McCall, Jr.
(1987, Stock #132) $65.00
Leadership for Turbulent Times L.R. Sayles (1995, Stock #325) $20.00
Learning How to Learn From Experience: Impact of Stress and Coping K.A. Bunker &
A.D. Webb (1992, Stock #154) $30.00
Making Common Sense: Leadership as Meaning-making in a Community of Practice
W.H. Drath & C.J. Palus (1994, Stock #156) $15.00
Off the Track: Why and How Successful Executives Get Derailed M.W. McCall, Jr., &
M.M. Lombardo (1983, Stock #121) $10.00
Preventing Derailment: What To Do Before It's Too Late M.M. Lombardo &
R.W. Eichinger (1989, Stock #138) $25.00
The Realities of Management Promotion M.N. Ruderman & P.J. Ohlott (1994, Stock #157) $20.00
Redefining What's Essential to Business Performance: Pathways to Productivity,
Quality, and Service L.R. Sayles (1990, Stock #142) $20.00
Succession Planning L.J. Eastman (1995, Stock #324) $20.00
Training for Action: A New Approach to Executive Development R.M. Burnside &
V.A. Guthrie (1992, Stock #153) $15.00
Traps and Pitfalls in the Judgment of Executive Potential M.N. Ruderman & P.J. Ohlott
(1990, Stock #141) $20.00
Twenty-two Ways to Develop Leadership in Staff Managers R.W. Eichinger & M.M. Lombardo
(1990, Stock #144) $15.00
Upward-communication Programs in American Industry A.I. Kraut & F.H. Freeman
(1992, Stock #152) $30.00
Using an Art Technique to Facilitate Leadership Development C. De Ciantis (1995, Stock #166)... $30.00
Why Executives Lose Their Balance J.R. Kofodimos (1989, Stock #137) $20.00

Why Managers Have Trouble Empowering: A Theoretical Perspective Based on Concepts of Adult Development W.H. Drath (1993, Stock #155) $15.00

SELECTED BOOKS:

Balancing Act: How Managers Can Integrate Successful Careers and Fulfilling Personal Lives J.R. Kofodimos (1993, Stock #247) $27.00

Beyond Ambition: How Driven Managers Can Lead Better and Live Better R.E. Kaplan, W.H. Drath, & J.R. Kofodimos (1991, Stock #227) $29.95

Breaking the Glass Ceiling: Can Women Reach the Top of America's Largest Corporations? (Updated Edition) A.M. Morrison, R.P. White, & E. Van Velsor (1992, Stock #236A) $12.50

Choosing to Lead K.E. Clark & M.B. Clark (1994, Stock #249) $35.00

Developing Diversity in Organizations: A Digest of Selected Literature A.M. Morrison & K.M. Crabtree (1992, Stock #317) $25.00

Discovering Creativity: Proceedings of the 1992 International Creativity and Innovation Networking Conference S.S. Gryskiewicz (Ed.) (1993, Stock #319) $30.00

Executive Selection: A Look at What We Know and What We Need to Know D.L. DeVries (1993, Stock #321) $20.00

Healing the Wounds: Overcoming the Trauma of Layoffs and Revitalizing Downsized Organizations D.M. Noer (1993, Stock #245) $26.00

If I'm In Charge Here, Why Is Everybody Laughing? D.P. Campbell (1980, Stock #205) $9.40

If You Don't Know Where You're Going You'll Probably End Up Somewhere Else D.P. Campbell (1974, Stock #203) $8.95

Inklings: Collected Columns on Leadership and Creativity D.P. Campbell (1992, Stock #233) $15.00

Leadership Education 1994-1995: A Source Book F.H. Freeman, K.B. Knott, & M.K. Schwartz (Eds.) (1994, Stock #322) $59.00

Leadership: Enhancing the Lessons of Experience R.L. Hughes, R.C. Ginnett, & G.J. Curphy (1992, Stock #246) $40.95

The Lessons of Experience: How Successful Executives Develop on the Job M.W. McCall, Jr., M.M. Lombardo, & A.M. Morrison (1988, Stock #211) $22.95

Making Diversity Happen: Controversies and Solutions A.M. Morrison, M.N. Ruderman, & M. Hughes-James (1993, Stock #320) $25.00

Measures of Leadership K.E. Clark & M.B. Clark (Eds.) (1990, Stock #215) $59.50

The New Leaders: Guidelines on Leadership Diversity in America A.M. Morrison (1992, Stock #238) $29.00

Readings in Innovation S.S. Gryskiewicz & D.A. Hills (Eds.) (1992, Stock #240) $25.00

Take the Road to Creativity and Get Off Your Dead End D.P. Campbell (1977, Stock #204) $8.95

Whatever It Takes: The Realities of Managerial Decision Making (Second Edition) M.W. McCall, Jr., & R.E. Kaplan (1990, Stock #218) $30.40

The Working Leader: The Triumph of High Performance Over Conventional Management Principles L.R. Sayles (1993, Stock #243) $24.95

SPECIAL PACKAGES:

Conversations with CEOs (includes 310 & 316) $16.00
Development & Derailment (includes 136, 138, & 144) $30.00
The Diversity Collection (includes 145, 236, 238, 317, & 320) $85.00
Executive Selection Package (includes 141, 321, & 157) $32.00
Feedback to Managers: Volumes I & II (includes 149 & 150) $85.00
Personal Growth, Taking Charge, and Enhancing Creativity (includes 203, 204, & 205) $20.00

Discounts are available. Please write for a comprehensive Publication & Products Catalog. Address your request to: Publication, Center for Creative Leadership, P.O. Box 26300, Greensboro, NC 27438-6300, 910-545-2805, or fax to 910-545-3221. All prices subject to change.

ORDER FORM

Name _____ Title _____

Organization _____

Mailing Address _____
(street address required for mailing)

City/State/Zip _____

Telephone _____ FAX _____
(telephone number required for UPS mailing)

Quantity	Stock No.	Title	Unit Cost	Amount
			Subtotal	
			Shipping and Handling (add 6% of subtotal with a $4.00 minimum; add 40% on all international shipping)	
			NC residents add 6% sales tax; CA residents add 7% sales tax; CO residents add 6.2% sales tax	
			TOTAL	

METHOD OF PAYMENT

❏ Check or money order enclosed (payable to Center for Creative Leadership).

❏ Purchase Order No. _____ (Must be accompanied by this form.)

❏ Charge my order, plus shipping, to my credit card:
   ❏ American Express   ❏ Discover   ❏ MasterCard   ❏ VISA

ACCOUNT NUMBER:_____ EXPIRATION DATE: MO.___ YR.___

NAME OF ISSUING BANK: _____

SIGNATURE _____

❏ Please put me on your mailing list.
❏ Please send me the Center's quarterly newsletter, *Issues & Observations*.

Publication • Center for Creative Leadership • P.O. Box 26300
Greensboro, NC 27438-6300
910-545-2805 • FAX 910-545-3221

Client Priority Code: R

fold here

PLACE
STAMP
HERE

CENTER FOR CREATIVE LEADERSHIP
PUBLICATION
P.O. Box 26300
Greensboro, NC 27438-6300